Why not try before you buy?

Download four free pages at swearybook.com/shithappens

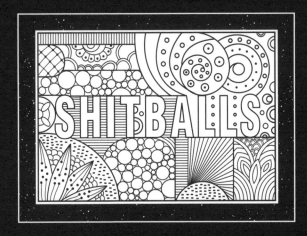

James Alexander

SHIT HAPPENS!

SWEAR WORDS AND MANTRAS TO COLOUR YOUR STRESS AWAY

Virgin BOOKS

Add yourself to the monthly newsletter
for free sweary downloads, news and
updates on forthcoming books
swearybook.com/newsletter

10 9 8 7 6 5 4 3 2 1

Virgin Books, an imprint of Ebury Publishing,
20 Vauxhall Bridge Road,
London SW1V 2SA

Virgin Books is part of the Penguin Random House group of companies
whose addresses can be found at global.penguinrandomhouse.com

 Penguin
Random House
UK

Copyright © James Alexander 2016

James Alexander has asserted his right to be identified as the author of this Work
in accordance with the Copyright, Designs and Patents Act 1988

First published by Virgin Books in 2016

www.eburypublishing.co.uk

A CIP catalogue record for this book is available from the British Library

ISBN 9780753545683

Design by Ben Gardiner
Printed and bound in Great Britain by Clays Ltd, St Ives PLC

Penguin Random House is committed to a sustainable future for our business, our readers
and our planet. This book is made from Forest Stewardship Council® certified paper.

MIX
Paper from
responsible sources
FSC® C018179

Dear Human,

Life can be full of surprises. Good surprises. Shitty surprises. When the going gets tough and you need to let out some steam, what do you do?

Introducing *Shit Happens!*, a new colouring book designed to help you relax and unwind with some choice words and bring a bit of laughter into your life!

Inside this colouring book, you'll find over thirty-five swear words, beautifully illustrated with intricate details, nature-inspired patterns and geometric shapes. Each single-sided page features a classic and wonderfully original insult, designed to help you unwind and let go of any challenges in your life.

Simply sit back, relax and choose the swear word that connects with you. Then colour in the details with your choice of colouring pencil, gel pen, marker and/or crayon. Because sometimes you just need to swear!

Enjoy the book!

James

P.S. Every month I give away free books and send out free colouring pages to members of my newsletter. You're invited! Head over to swearybook.com and add yourself to the list.

Looking for more colourful language?

Receive more sweary designs in printable PDF format.
Download for free here at swearybook.com/secretdesigns

Fuck yeah!

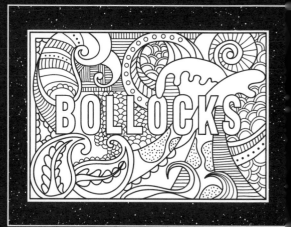

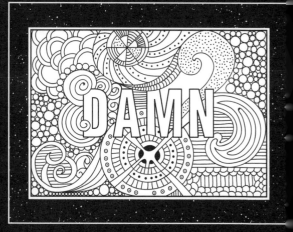